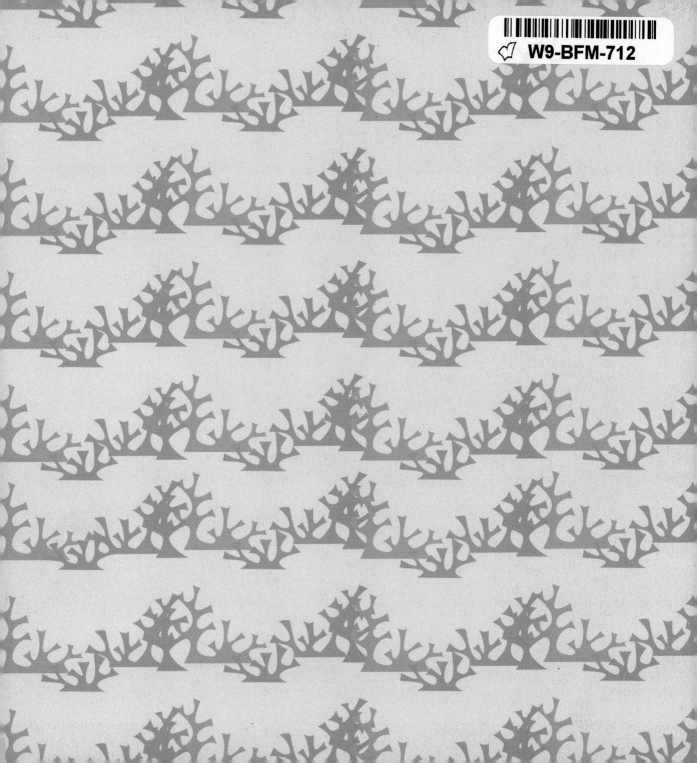

UNDERSEA SCHOOL

Disney · PIXAR

FINDING NEMO

Tales of Whales
and other Amazing Ocean Mammals

by Kathleen Kranking

Scholastic Inc.
New York · Toronto · London · Auckland · Sydney
Mexico City · New Delhi · Hong Kong · Buenos Aires

For Carlyn and Maren,
two of my favorite mammals

Cover Designer: Aruna Goldstein
Designer: Julia Sarno
Interior illustrations: Yancey Labat

Photo Credits:
Cover: (blue whale) © David B. Fleetham/SeaPics.com.
Page 6-7: (background) © Jeff Hunter/Photographer's Choice/Getty Images.
Page 8-9: (background) © Darryl Torckler/Stone/Getty Images.
Page 12-13: (sei whale) © Doug Perrine/SeaPics.com; (background) © Stuart Westmorland/The Image Bank/Getty Images.
Page 12: (humpback whale) © Michael Melford/The Image Bank/ Getty Images.
Page 13: (whale tail) © James Gritz/Photodisc Green (RF)/Getty Images; (whale spouting) © Phillip Colla/SeaPics.com
Page 14-15: (background–rippled water, full frame, underwater view) © Ken Usami/Photodisc Red (RF)/ Getty Images.
Page 15: (humpback whale (Novaeangliae megaptera) swimming in South Pacific) © Pete Atkinson/Taxi/Getty Images;
          (humpback whale breaching) © Doug Perrine/SeaPics.com.
Page 16-17: (background) © Richard Herrmann/SeaPics.com.
Page 16: (mother humpback & calf) @ Amos Nachoum/The Image Bank/ Getty Images.
Page 17: (baleen) © Phillip Colla/SeaPics.com; (baleen of right whale) © Armin Maywald/SeaPics.com
Page 18: (blue whale) © Mike Johnson/SeaPics.com; (humpback whale) © David Fleetham/ Photographer's Choice/Getty Images;
          (gray whale) © Howard Hall/SeaPics.com; (bowhead whale) © Doc White/SeaPics.com.
Page 19: (sperm whale with squid) © Richard Ellis/SeaPics.com; (beluga whale) © Jonathan Bird/SeaPics.com;
          (narwhal whales) © Goran Ehlme/SeaPics.com.
Page 21: (background) © Stephen Frink /The Image Bank/ Getty Images; (dolphin) © David B. Fleetham/SeaPics.com;
          (porpoise) © Florian Graner/SeaPics.com; (jumping dolphin) © SBI/NASA Taxi /Getty Images.
Page 22-23: (background) Diver's exhaust bubbles © Stephen Frink /The Image Bank/Getty Images.
Page 22: (dolphin pod) © image100 (RF)/ Getty Images; (dolphin mother & calf) © Doug Perrine/SeaPics.com.
Page 23: (amazon river dolphin) © Gregory Ochocki/SeaPics.com; (bottlenose dolphin, caribbean) © James Gritz/Photodisc Green (RF)/Getty Images;
          (spinner dolphin) © James D. Watt/SeaPics.com; (spotted dolphin) © Jeff Hunter /The Image Bank/Getty Images.
Page 24: (orca whale) © David Fleetham/Taxi/Getty Images.
Page 25: (background) © Ken Usami/ Photodisc Red (RF)/Getty Images; (seal) © James D. Watt/SeaPics.com; (sea lion) © Tim Laman /National Geographic/
          Getty Images.
Page 26-27: (background) © Ken Usami/ Photodisc Red (RF)/Getty Images.
Page 26: (harbor seal) © Royalty-Free/Corbis; (mother harp seal & pup) Harp Seal Kissing Whitecoat Seal © Brakefield Photo / Brand X Pictures (RF)/
          Getty Images.
Page 27: (sea lions on beach) © Geostock/Photodisc Green (RF)/Getty Images.
Page 28-29: (background) © Ihoko Saito/Toshiyuki Tajima (RF)/Getty Images .
Page 28: (walrus tusks) © Royalty-Free/Corbis; (fighting walruses) © Kevin Schafer/SeaPics.com.
Page 29: (snuggling walruses) © Mirnottito / Digital Vision (RF)/Getty Images; (walrus whiskers) © Saul Gonor/SeaPics.com.
Page 30: (manatee eating) Manatee Eating Lettuce Underwater © Royalty-Free/Corbis; (manatee & diver) © Phillip Colla/SeaPics.com.
Page 31: (manatee) © Doug Perrine/SeaPics.com; (dugong) © Doug Perrine/SeaPics.com; (west indian manatee) © Phillip Colla/SeaPics.com.
Page 32-33: (background) © Larry Gatz/The Image Bank/ Getty Images.
Page 32: (sea otters) © Johnny Johnson/Photographer's Choice / Getty Images.
Page 33: (sea otter with rock) © Hal Beral/V&W/SeaPics.com; (sea otter in kelp) © Doc White/SeaPics.com.
Page 34: (polar bear swimming) © Sea world Of California/Corbis; (three polar bears) © Larry Williams/Corbis.
Page 36: (dolphins spy-hopping) © Susan Dabritz-Yuen/SeaPics.com.
Page 37: (background) © Darryl Torckler/Stone/Getty Images.

Published by Scholastic Inc., 557 Broadway, New York, NY 10012, by arrangement
with Disney Licensed Publishing. SCHOLASTIC, UNDERSEA SCHOOL, and
associated logos are trademarks and/or registered trademarks of Scholastic Inc.

ISBN 0-439-79884-1

12 11 10 9 8 7 6 5 4 3 2 1   5 6 7 8 9 10/0

Printed in the U.S.A.
First Scholastic printing, July 2005

Table of Contents

Get ready for a whale of a good time!

Nemo
clown fish

Hi, there! It's me, Nemo! I'm back here at Undersea School waiting for you to join me on a very BIG adventure. Are you ready to visit with some of the largest creatures in the ocean? We're going to hang out with huge whales, giant walruses, enormous manatees, and lots of our other ocean friends.

But guess what? Even though I live in the ocean with all these animals, you really have more in common with them than I do! Sound a little fishy? Well, there's really nothing fishy about it—because none of them are fish. They're all mammals—just like you!

Here's a sneak peek at the animals we'll meet:

- whales that sing songs,

- seals that bark like dogs,

- walruses with super-long tusks,

- and otters that use tools!

DORY
blue tang

Hello there, mammal! I'm Dory. I'm a fish. Hey…have we met? I'm Dory.

Mammals that live in the ocean can do a lot of really cool things. Let's get ready to make some amazing mammal discoveries! In this adventure, we'll find out:

- **how whales keep warm,**

- **what manatees like to eat,**

- **how smart dolphins are,**

- **and a whole lot more!**

Take a deep breath and dive right in! It's time to meet the mammals!

Chapter 1: Make Way for Mammals

So, what exactly is a mammal? Mammals are a group of animals that are alike in the following five ways:

1. *Most of them have hair. (A few don't, like whales.)*
2. *They use lungs to breathe air.*
3. *Most give birth to live young, instead of laying eggs like some animals.*
4. *Mammal mothers nurse their babies with milk.*
5. *They are warm-blooded.*

crush
sea turtle

Temperature Talk

Hey there, dudes! Crush here, to make something clear. You're probably, like, "Whoa, what's all this warm-blooded stuff?" Well, here's the scoop. When an animal is warm-blooded, its body stays the same warm temperature all the time. But cold-blooded animals, like me and my fishy-type friends, are different. If the water around us is warm, we heat up. If the water around us is cold...we chill! It's totally righteous!

Can you name one difference between fish and mammals?

Fish breathe underwater. Mammals need to breathe air.

Breathe air? Ewww!

Sheldon
sea horse

Tad
butterfly fish

The Marine Scene

Mammals that live in the ocean are called marine mammals. They include whales, dolphins, seals, sea lions, walruses, manatees, sea otters, and others. Marine mammals have everything they need to survive in their watery world. By the end of our adventure, you'll have a deep understanding of all of them! So let's get started by swimming to the next page. It's time to meet some whales!

CLOWNING AROUND!

Q: Do you know what marine mammals like to do best at a playground?

A: Ride the "sea-saw!"

Marlin
clown fish

Chapter 2: Wise Up About Whales

You know, it might seem that a mammal in the ocean would be like...well...a fish out of water! That would be true for a land mammal, but a marine mammal is specially built for undersea life.

Body Basics

A *whale's* body is perfectly shaped for gliding along through the ocean. With its streamlined shape—kind of like a torpedo—it can move easily through the water. And its sleek skin helps make for smooth sailing, as well. Some whales are speedy swimmers. Sei whales, like the one below, can swim up to 23 miles (37 km) per hour.

sei whale

> ### Clowning Around!
>
> **Q:** What does a whale do at the end of a race?
> **A:** It crosses the *fin*-ish line!

The ocean can be a very cold place to live. Without a coat of fur to keep warm, what's a whale to do? Don't worry, whales have it covered—with blubber. Blubber is a thick layer of fat just under a whale's skin. It's like a built-in blanket to keep whales warm. Some whales have a blubber layer that's thicker than a mattress!

humpback whale

whale tail

A Tale of a Tail

A whale's tail is super-strong and it gets the whale where it wants to go. Whales move their tails in big up-and-down strokes to swim. But fish swim by moving their tails from side to side. I guess it's different strokes for different folks!

Way to Blow!

Whales need to come to the surface to get air. At the surface, a whale blows a blast of air out of its blowhole on the top of its head. This is called spouting. Then the whale takes a big breath in through its blowhole, closes it up, and dives back down into the water. Sperm whales can hold their breath for more than an hour!

whale spouting

Good Earsight?

The deeper a whale goes into the ocean, the darker it gets. So, many kinds of whales have a sense called *echolocation*. That means they use echoes to find things, such as their food. With echolocation a whale can tell the size, shape, and speed of an object, as well as the direction in which it's moving. It's like the whale can *see* by listening!

That's a Mouthful, Mate!

G'day, mate! Let's take a bite out of the word: *echolocation* (ECK-oh-loh-CAY-shun). Echolocation allows some kinds of whales to locate objects in the ocean using sound waves. Here's how it works: First, a whale sends out clicking sounds that it makes inside its head. When the sounds hit something, they bounce back as echoes. By listening to the echoes, the whale can "see" the object in the dark ocean. I wish I could do that, mate. I could use echoes to locate some nice, juicy, uh, friends. Yeah, that's it. Fish are friends, not food!

BRUCE
great white shark

whale using echolocation

A whale of a racket

Whales make some very loud noises!

Clicks, whistles, chirps, moans, roars, pops, and lots of other sounds are all types of "whale talk" and "whale singing."

A whale doesn't make noises from its throat like you do. Instead, it makes sounds from a place inside its head, beneath its blowhole. Male humpback whales are famous for their singing. With their heads pointed down into the water, they can sing for hours.

humpback whale

Breach for the sky

You know that whales are good at diving *in* the water. But some of them are good at diving *out* of the water! Many whales breach. That means they make a giant leap into the air, then slam back down against the water with a big splash. And a big noise! Scientists think whales breach to send messages to other whales. Of course, only the whales know for sure! Hey, maybe Dory can ask them...

I speeeeaaaaak whaaaaaaaale.

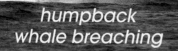
humpback whale breaching

15

Baby Talk

Whales have some of the biggest babies in the world! A mother whale usually has just one baby, or calf, at a time. When a calf is born, its mother lifts it up to the surface to breathe. The calf soon learns to breathe on its own.

mother humpback whale with her calf

You have more in common with whale calves than you might think. Their parents sometimes give them piggyback rides, just as yours might. And some of them even have babysitters! When a mother sperm whale needs to dive deep to get food, other female sperm whales watch over her baby.

On the Move

Each year many whales *migrate* from their feeding grounds to warmer water when they're ready to have their babies. How do they get ready for their trip? They spend all summer eating! Blue whales might eat two tons of food a day! All this eating builds up their blubber layers, so whales can live on their fat during their travels. Some whales can swim up to a hundred miles a day without eating!

That's a Mouthful, Mate!

Animals *migrate* when they travel from one place to another. They usually do this to get to feeding places or places to have their young.

CHUM
mako shark

The scoop on Baleen

When it comes to eating, there are two kinds of whales: hungry and hungrier! Just kidding! But, there really are two kinds of whales—baleen whales and toothed whales—and they have very different ways of eating. Almost all the biggest whales belong to the baleen group, which is funny because baleen whales eat the smallest kinds of food!

baleen

Baleen whales don't have any teeth. Instead they have strips of baleen, which hang down like a curtain from the roof of their mouths. The baleen is bristly, kind of like a hairbrush, and is made of the same stuff as your fingernails. Baleen traps plankton, including shrimp-like animals called krill.

Here's how baleen works: The whale opens its mouth wide and takes in a lot of water. Then it closes its mouth, forcing the water back out through the baleen. The tiny creatures are trapped inside the baleen as the water drains out. Then the whale swallows them. *Gulp!*

The right whale has very long strips of baleen. Its baleen can be three times as long as you are tall!

baleen of a right whale

Let's scoop up some neat facts about baleen whales!

The blue whale is bigger than any animal in the world. A full-grown blue whale is about as long as three school buses parked end to end! In one day, it eats about 40 million krill.

blue whale

humpback whale

Humpback whales also eat krill, but some of them have a trick for catching schools of fish. They blow bubbles in the water to make a kind of wall around the fish. Then the humpbacks plow into the school with open mouths. Chow time!

gray whale

Gray whales are the best long-distance swimmers of all the whales. In one year, a gray whale can swim up to 14,000 miles (22,530 km). That's like swimming back and forth across the United States more than three times!

bowhead whale

Most whales live about 50 to 70 years. But the bowhead has been known to live more than a hundred years!

CLOWNING AROUND!

Q: What's longer than a blue whale?

A: Two blue whales!

Toothy-Type Whales

Now that we've spent some time with baleen whales, let's meet the toothed whales. These whales have teeth that they use to chow down on fish, squid, and even some mammals.

Sperm whales are the biggest of all the toothed whales. Some can dive more than a mile deep and can hold their breath for more than an hour! Down in the dark depths, they find one of their favorite meals—the giant squid.

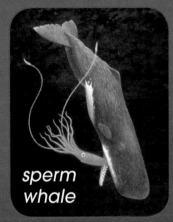
sperm whale

beluga whale

The beluga whale is one of the most talkative whales. People call it the "sea canary" because it makes so many different sounds, including chirps, squeaks, whistles, and even moos!

The male narwhal whale has a long tooth that grows right through its lip and forms a tusk. It's easy to see why narwhals are called "unicorns of the sea."

narwhal whales

Nice swimming, so far! We're going to wave good-bye to these whales and drop in on the dolphins—but first, let's take a break with some Fishy Fun. Bzzzzzzzzzzz! There's the recess bell...let's go!

FISHY FUN: An A-MAZE-ing Journey

This humpback whale needs to get to warmer water, where she can join her friends and give birth to her baby. Can you help her find the way?

(When you're done with your journey, turn to page 38.)

Chapter 3: Discover Dolphins

Let's dive into some splish-splashy fun with the *dolphins*! Dolphins are toothed whales that have long snouts and slender bodies. They live in all the world's oceans, except the coldest ones near the North and South Poles. Are you ready to take a swim with them? Let's go!

A clue to who's who

Dolphins are close cousins of *porpoises*. Can you guess which of the animals to the right is a dolphin and which is a porpoise? A dolphin has a pointy nose, called a beak, and a porpoise has no beak. So, if you said the dolphin is on top, you're right on the nose! Porpoises also have a shorter top fin and flatter teeth than dolphins do.

bottlenose dolphin

Dancing Dolphins

Do you like doing somersaults? If you could do them in midair, you'd make a good dolphin! Dolphins can jump like gymnasts and spin like ballerinas. Some even like to hitch rides on the big waves made by boats.

Dolphin Details

Most dolphins live in groups called pods. Some pods are made up of mother dolphins and their calves, others of "teenage" dolphins, and still others of older male dolphins. Sometimes many pods travel together, forming a herd of hundreds of dolphins!

dolphin pod

a dolphin mother and her calf

Dolphins identify themselves by making whistling sounds. Each dolphin has its very own whistle, which it learns from its mother. By hearing each other's whistles, dolphins can tell who's who in their pod. If a calf and its mother get separated, they both keep whistling until they find each other.

Dolphin Smarts

If dolphins went to Undersea School, they'd probably be the best students in the class—except for you, of course! Dolphins are very intelligent and have great memories, which is why they're so good at learning tricks. Some dolphins have been taught a form of sign language. They learned the meanings of words and could even understand sentences. One dolphin learned the meaning of more than 60 words!

CLOWNING AROUND!

Q: Why couldn't the dolphin finish its book?

A: It kept flipping back to the beginning!

Now that you've learned about dolphins, let's make some new dolphin friends!

The Amazon River dolphin has pink skin! River dolphins are the only dolphins that live in freshwater rivers. Since this dolphin has very poor eyesight, it depends on echolocation to find fish and other food.

Amazon River dolphin

bottlenose dolphin

Bottlenose dolphins are probably the most well-known dolphins, since they are often seen doing tricks in marine park shows. They live in warm oceans all around the world.

After leaping out of the water, the spinner dolphin spins around and around like a top in midair. The spinning may be a way of communicating with other dolphins, or "spinning off" tiny pests on its skin.

spinner dolphin

spotted dolphin

A spotted dolphin has to grow into its name! Newborn spotted dolphins don't have any spots at all. But as they get older, spots appear on their bellies and spread all over their bodies.

We've already learned that dolphins are toothed whales. But did you know that the largest dolphin is the killer whale? (You can't always judge a dolphin by its name!) Killer whales can grow to about 30 feet—as long as two minivans!

There are two types of killer whales. The first type eats mostly fish. These killer whales chase a school of fish until they're trapped against the shore. Then they gobble them up! The second type of killer whale eats seals and seabirds, like penguins. Sometimes a group of killer whales will even attack and eat other whales—from smaller dolphins to blue whales that are three times as big as they are!

That big white oval shape on the killer whale's head looks like an eye, but it's just a patch of color. The real eye is in front of the white patch and much smaller.

🐟 🐟 Something's Fishy 🐟 🐟 🐟 🐟 🐟

Pssst. What do you think of the name *killer whale*? I like it. It sounds tough! But others think this name is misleading because it makes these dolphins sound mean. After all, killer whales only attack other animals because they're hungry, just like any other predator. So some people think it's better to call killer whales by their other name: orcas.

Gill
moorish idol

24

Chapter 4: Swimming with Seals and Sea Lions

Seals and *sea lions* are at home both on land and at sea. Most of them live in colder parts of the ocean, but some live in warmer waters along the coasts. They eat mostly fish and squid, though some like other kinds of food, such as shellfish or seabirds.

The Deal on Seals and Sea Lions

If a seal and a sea lion came swimming up to you, would you be able to tell them apart? Here are some things to check for:

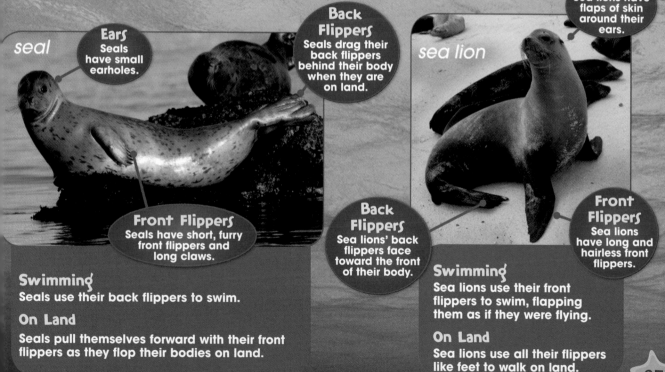

seal

Ears
Seals have small earholes.

Back Flippers
Seals drag their back flippers behind their body when they are on land.

Front Flippers
Seals have short, furry front flippers and long claws.

Swimming
Seals use their back flippers to swim.

On Land
Seals pull themselves forward with their front flippers as they flop their bodies on land.

sea lion

Ears
Sea lions have flaps of skin around their ears.

Back Flippers
Sea lions' back flippers face toward the front of their body.

Front Flippers
Sea lions have long and hairless front flippers.

Swimming
Sea lions use their front flippers to swim, flapping them as if they were flying.

On Land
Sea lions use all their flippers like feet to walk on land.

25

Well-Built for Water

Seals and sea lions are graceful swimmers. Like whales, they keep warm in the water with a thick layer of blubber under their skin. They also have fur coats. Each year they shed their coats and grow sleek new ones.

Like all marine mammals, seals and sea lions must come to the surface to breathe air. They take a breath through their nose. Then, just before they dive back under, their nostrils automatically snap shut to keep water out. And when a seal or sea lion opens its mouth underwater to grab a fish or other food, the back of its throat closes. That way it doesn't swallow a lot of water.

harbor seal

Nigel
pelican

Hi, there! I'm Nigel. Since I can get a bird's-eye view of seals and sea lions on land, Nemo asked me to fly over and tell you about them!

Living on Land

When spring comes, seals and sea lions leave their watery world to come ashore. Why? Because it's time for babies to be born! Baby seals are called pups. They drink their mothers' warm milk and grow and grow. Seal milk is very fatty. It's as thick as a milk shake. That fatty milk becomes blubber that will keep the pups warm.

mother harp seal and pup

A seal and sea lion's land life can get pretty crowded—and noisy! Males may battle each other to see who's boss. And mothers and pups often call to each other. Most seals and sea lions communicate by barking. Some of them gather in groups of hundreds—or even thousands. That's a pretty big pack of *pinnipeds*!

sea lions on a beach

That's a Mouthful, Mate!

Seals and sea lions have flippers for feet. They belong to a group called *pinnipeds* (PIN-uh-peds), which means "fin-footed."

Anchor
hammerhead shark

CLOWNING AROUND!

Q: What is a seal's favorite kind of boat?

A: *Ark! Ark!*

Well, I've gotta fly, and since Nemo's on his way back, I'll say bye-bye! Hey, that reminds me of a joke: How did the pelican say good-bye to the fish? "Catch you later!"

Let's leave the jokes to the clown fish, okay?

27

Chapter 5: What's Up with Walruses?

Now it's time to meet another pinniped: the big, whiskery *walrus*. Walruses live in the icy, cold ocean around the North Pole. Like seals and sea lions, they spend some of their time on land. When they pull themselves out of the water, it's onto the ice! Luckily, they have thick blubber to keep them warm.

What Big Teeth They Have

A walrus's sharp tusks are actually teeth. But they don't use them for chewing. They use their tusks as:

- *Ice picks:* Tusks come in handy for poking breathing holes into the ice. Since walruses often swim under the ice, breathing holes give them a place to come up for air.

- *Arms:* A walrus uses its tusks to help pull itself out of the water.

- *Weapons:* Males sometimes stab each other with their tusks when they fight. Their thick skin protects them.

- *Anchors:* Sometimes walruses in the water will hook their tusks onto the ice so they can take a snooze without slipping into the water.

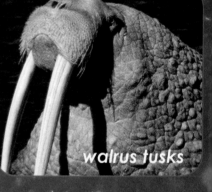

walrus tusks

fighting walruses

snuggling walruses

You'd think with those sharp tusks sticking out, the last thing walruses would want to do is snuggle! But snuggling is a way for them to keep warm in their cold Arctic home. When walruses warm up in the sun, tiny blood vessels in their skin fill with blood. That makes them look pink!

Did you know that both male and female walruses have tusks?

A walrus's tusks keep growing all its life. They can be as long as a person's arm!

squirt
sea turtle

Feeling for Food

When a walrus is hungry, it dives down to the ocean floor. It's hard to see in the dark, murky depths, but that's no problem! A walrus has a bushy bunch of super-sensitive whiskers that look like a mustache. It uses them like fingers to feel around on the bottom. When the walrus finds a clam, snail, or other food, it uses its tough-skinned snout to dig it out.

walrus whiskers

But if food, like a clam, is buried very deep, the walrus has another trick. It squirts a mouthful of water right at it, blasting it out of the sand. Then it sucks the clam out of its shell.

Chapter 6: Meet the Manatees

Want to hear something funny? A long time ago, sailors used to spot *manatees* in the water and think they were mermaids! It's hard to imagine why. To me they look more like big, gray marshmallows with flippers!

Manatees spend their entire lives in the water. They don't have as much blubber as some other marine mammals. So they live in warmer parts of the ocean and also swim up into warm freshwater rivers.

Munching Machines

Unlike zipping seals and flipping dolphins, manatees live slow, quiet lives. They aren't speedy swimmers, but that's fine for them. They never have to chase their food—they only eat plants! A manatee can eat a hundred pounds of plants a day!

manatee eating plants

Gentle Giants

Manatees are peaceful, gentle animals. They're graceful when they're swimming—gliding and turning in the water like roly-poly ballerinas! Manatees talk to each other with high chirps and squeaks. And they even greet each other with what look like kisses! When manatees see people in the

manatee and a diver

water, they'll sometimes swim over and nuzzle them with their whiskery lips. And they seem to like having their bellies rubbed, too!

Manatee Family

Dugongs are cousins to manatees. Want to know how to tell them apart? Here's a hint: Take a look at their tails. Manatees have rounded tails that are shaped like paddles. Dugongs have tails that look like whales' tails. Want to know something else? Manatees and dugongs are the only marine mammals that eat just plants.

manatee

dugong

Chessie must've known my favorite song: Just keep swimming... just keep swimming...

A Manatee's Journey

The kind of manatee that lives closest to the United States is the West Indian manatee. It lives along the coast of Florida. Sometimes these manatees swim a little farther north in the summer because the water gets warmer there. One West Indian manatee became famous for doing something very unusual. This manatee, nicknamed Chessie, swam north and kept going... and going...and going! He just kept swimming until he got all the way to Rhode Island! Then he turned around and swam all the way back to Florida!

West Indian manatee

Chapter 7: Spy On Sea Otters

Hey, look! It's a pair of furry *sea otters*! Sea otters are the smallest of all the marine mammals. They live in the northern Pacific Ocean along rocky coasts and in kelp forests. (Kelp is a kind of tall seaweed that grows up from the ocean floor.) Let's take a swim with the sea otters!

sea otters

A Whole Lot of Hair

Sea otters may be the smallest of all the sea mammals, but they're the hairiest animals in the whole world! A sea otter doesn't have a blubber layer to keep it warm in the cold water. Instead, it has extra-thick fur to do the job—with a million hairs on every square inch of its body. You have only about one-tenth that amount on your whole head!

The otter's fur traps a layer of air against its body. And that layer of air blocks out the water. So even though the otter is swimming, its skin never gets wet! Since dirty, matted fur won't keep out the water, otters spend many hours a day cleaning themselves by rolling in the water and rubbing their fur with their paws. Rub and roll, roll and rub—that's the sea otter way to scrub!

CLOWNING AROUND!

Q: Why did the sea otter cross the ocean?

A: To get to the *otter* side!

There *otter* be a law against bad otter jokes!

It's cool to use a tool

The sea otter does something no other marine mammal does. It uses a rock as a tool to get its food. A sea otter eats oysters, clams, crabs, sea urchins, and other animals that have hard shells. To break the shell, the sea otter floats on its back, puts a rock on its chest, and then whacks the food against the rock until the shell cracks open.

sea otter with rock

> Sea otters have pouches of skin under their front legs. They use them as built-in pockets for holding rocks—kind of like an otter-type tool belt! Awesome!

That's a wrap

Sea otters live where there's lots of kelp. When an otter wants to sleep, it wraps itself in kelp so it won't drift away. And when an otter mom needs to look for food, she'll wrap her baby in kelp to keep it safe until she comes back.

sea otter wrapped in kelp

What About Polar Bears?

Are you surprised to see a *polar bear* here? Even though polar bears don't spend as much time in the water as other marine mammals, they're still right at home in the sea. Polar bears are actually considered marine mammals, and their scientific name even means "sea bear"!

Polar bears live in the frozen lands around the North Pole. Thick fur and lots of blubber keep them warm in the icy water. Polar bears are great swimmers and can swim ten miles (16 km) without stopping! They also find their favorite meals in the water—like a nice, juicy seal or beluga whale.

Great work! You've swum a long way and learned a lot about all kinds of marine mammals. Are you ready to give your flippers a break and dive into more Fishy Fun? Let's go!

FISHY FUN: Crack this SEA-cret Code

Here's a riddle for you: What is a seal's favorite game to play on land? To find out the answer, complete the sentences below by filling in the blanks. If you need help, turn back to pages 25–33. Once you have all the answers filled in, write the letters that have marine mammals under them in the correct boxes at the bottom of the page. Good luck! *(When you've cracked the code, turn to page 38.)*

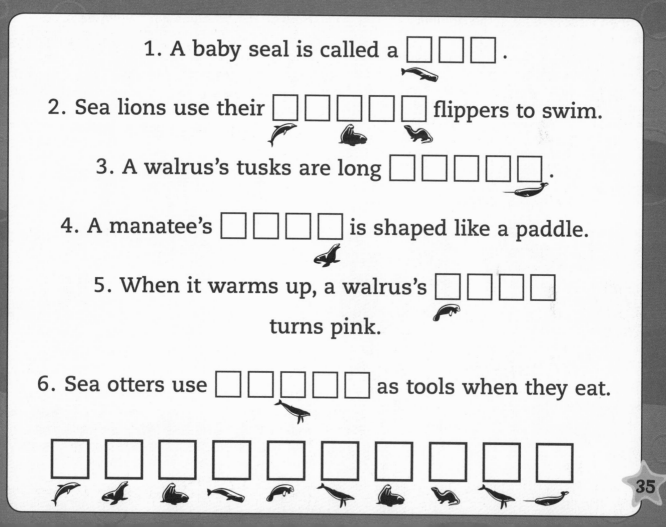

1. A baby seal is called a ☐☐☐ .

2. Sea lions use their ☐☐☐☐☐ flippers to swim.

3. A walrus's tusks are long ☐☐☐☐☐ .

4. A manatee's ☐☐☐☐ is shaped like a paddle.

5. When it warms up, a walrus's ☐☐☐☐ turns pink.

6. Sea otters use ☐☐☐☐☐ as tools when they eat.

☐☐☐☐☐☐☐☐☐☐

SHOW·AND·TELL

with Oceanarium Director, Cheryl Messinger

Want to meet my new friend? Her name is Cheryl Messinger, and she has a really neat job! She is the director of a place called The Dolphin Connection in the Florida Keys. That's a place where kids and grown-ups can learn about dolphins in a special way—by petting and playing with them!

What do visitors learn at the Dolphin Connection?

CHERYL: We teach people how important it is to take care of the ocean, because dolphins and other sea animals need a clean, healthy ocean to survive. We feel that if people meet our dolphins and see how neat they are, that will inspire them to care about the ocean and the animals in it. Our educational programs allow people to get in the water with the dolphins. They can touch them, hug them, kiss them, and get to know them. We also tell them that it's okay to feed dolphins at a zoo or aquarium, but it's dangerous to feed dolphins in the wild. They can get sick.

Can you tell me about the dolphins you have?

CHERYL: There are six dolphins, which live in a penned-off part of the ocean. Our two adult females are named April and Allie. There are two male calves, Wilson and Balla. And there are two adult males named Sebastian and Nemo.

Hey—just like me!

CHERYL: That's right!

Nemo the dolphin

How do the dolphins act toward people?

CHERYL: Our dolphins love attention from people! About five or ten minutes before the program starts, they spy-hop, which means they poke their heads out of the water and look for the visitors. As the people wade into the water, the dolphins swim right up to them.

dolphins spy-hopping

How is your research helpful to wild dolphins?

CHERYL: Researchers that work in the wild and at zoos and aquariums share information that helps all different kinds of animals. Our dolphins let us collect information from them, and this helps us learn more about dolphins that live in human care and dolphins that live in the wild.

What is your favorite part of your job?

CHERYL: My favorite part is spending time with the dolphins and also being able to share the dolphins with people. I see the admiration, respect, and awe people have for the dolphins when they leave. To be able to give people that experience is just incredible.

School's Out!

Well, our undersea adventure has been great fun, don't you think? We've really learned a lot. You've become a whiz at whales and walruses, an expert on echolocation, and a student of seals and sea otters. There's lots more fun to come at Undersea School. We'll meet more amazing undersea animals and travel to cool and colorful places in the ocean!

But for now, you'd better get dried off. I think I hear the school bell! It's time to go home!

Join us next time for more adventures in Undersea School!

Let's make like the ocean and wave!

Hello, welcome to Undersea School! Oh, I mean good-bye! See you later!

37

NEMO'S ANSWER PAGE

Fishy Fun:
An A-MAZE-ing Journey
(page 20)

Did you help the humpback whale find her way to warmer water? Let's see which way she went...

Fishy Fun:
Crack this SEA-cret Code
(page 35)

Were you able to crack the code?

1. A baby seal is called a P U P .

2. Sea lions use their F R O N T flippers to swim.

3. A walrus's tusks are long T E E T H .

4. A manatee's T A I L is shaped like a paddle.

5. When it warms up, a walrus's S K I N turns pink.

6. Sea otters use R O C K S as tools when they eat.

F L O P S C O T C H